TOP 10
PROFESSIONAL
BASKETBALL
COACHES

Ron Knapp

Enslow Publishers, Inc.

44 Fadem Road   PO Box 38
Box 699   Aldershot
Springfield, NJ 07081   Hants GU12 6BP
USA   UK

RYL FP CDS JY Jm RM

Copyright © 1998 by Ron Knapp

Library of Congress Cataloging-in-Publication Data

Knapp, Ron.
    Top 10 professional basketball coaches / Ron Knapp.
        p. cm. — (Sports top 10)
    Includes bibliographical references (p.) and index.
    Summary: Profiles the lives and careers of Red Auerbach, Chuck Daly, Alex
Hannum, Red Holzman, Phil Jackson, John Kundla, Don Nelson, Pat Riley, Bill
Russell, and Rudy Tomjanovich.
    ISBN 0-7660-1008-2
    1. Basketball coaches—United States—Biography—Juvenile literature.
2. Basketball coaches—Rating of—United States—Juvenile literature.
[1. Basketball coaches.] I. Title. II. Series.
GV884.A1K638   1998
796.323'092273—dc21
[B]   97-21634
                                           CIP
                                         AC

Printed in the United States of America

10 9 8 7 6 5 4 3 2 1

Illustration Credits: AP/Wide World Photos, pp. 7, 15, 17, 21, 29, 38;
© Mitchell Layton, pp. 10, 13, 22, 25, 30, 33, 34, 37, 42, 45; Naismith
Memorial Basketball Hall of Fame, pp. 9, 19, 27, 41.

Cover Illustration: © Mitchell Layton.

Interior Design: Richard Stalzer

CONTENTS

Introduction

FOR MANY YOUNG FANS TODAY, professional basketball is their favorite sport. Players like Michael Jordan and Hakeem Olajuwon have become superstars, earning millions of dollars every season. Their names and pictures seem to be everywhere—on posters, books, clothing, and shoes.

Of course, it's men like Jordan and Olajuwon who get the credit for making the National Basketball Association (NBA) so incredibly popular. They're the ones who make the dunks, grab the rebounds, and block the shots.

But where would the superstars be without their coaches? One-man teams rarely win championships. The squads that work well together take home the trophies. Someone has to come up with strategies and provide the leadership to keep the teams running smoothly—and winning. That's the job of the coaches.

The coaches in this book are ten very different men. Some of them have been dictators who made all the crucial decisions themselves. Others have welcomed suggestions from their players and assistants. Some of them treated their players as friends; others went out of their way to be disliked.

Most of these men were once NBA players themselves. One of them, Bill Russell, was still playing nearly every minute of almost every important game when he was coaching his team to glory.

Some of these men have become almost as famous—and nearly as rich—as their players. Any fan who knows anything about the great teams of the NBA will remember Red Auerbach's cigars. Before you opened this book, you probably already knew about Pat Riley's slicked-back hairstyle.

But, despite their success, some of these men have been forgotten. How many young fans realize that the league's most successful team was once the Minneapolis Lakers? Or that their brilliant coach was a young man named John Kundla?

Despite their differences, these coaches are all winners. Altogether, they've won 31 NBA titles. Whatever they've tried with their teams has worked.

CAREER STATISTICS

Coach	Teams	Years	Wins	Losses	Pct.
RED AUERBACH	Capitols, Blackhawks, Celtics	1946–47 to 1965–66	938	479	.662
CHUCK DALY	Cavaliers, Pistons, Nets, Magic	1981–82; 1983–84 to 1993–94; 1997–98—	564	379	.598
ALEX HANNUM	Hawks, Nationals, Warriors, 76ers, Rockets	1956–57 to 1957–58; 1960–61 to 1967–68; 1969–70 to 1970–71	471	412	.533
RED HOLZMAN	Hawks, Knicks	1953–54 to 1956–57; 1967–68 to 1981–82	696	604	.535
PHIL JACKSON	Bulls	1989–90—	483	173	.736
JOHN KUNDLA	Lakers	1948–49 to 1950–51 1951–52 to 1958–59	423	302	.583
DON NELSON	Bucks, Warriors, Knicks, Mavericks	1976–77 to 1986–87; 1988–89 to 1995–96; 1997–98—	851	630	.575
PAT RILEY	Lakers, Knicks, Heat	1981–82 to 1989–90; 1991–92	859	360	.705
BILL RUSSELL	Celtics, SuperSonics, Kings	1966–67 to 1968–69; 1973–74 to 1976–77; 1987–88	341	290	.540
RUDY TOMJANOVICH	Rockets	1991–92—	281	159	.639

Chart only includes NBA statistics through 1996–97 season.

Red Auerbach

No COACH HAS EVER BEEN AS DISLIKED—or as successful—as Red Auerbach. When his Boston Celtics were safely ahead late in a game, he would light a victory cigar and begin smoking it on the bench. In Boston, the fans loved it, but in other towns, the crowds felt he was rubbing the defeat in their faces.

Auerbach was never concerned about being popular with the fans—or with his players. One of his secrets, he said, was being rough on his team: "If you get obnoxious, you build incentive."[1] He made his players work hard. "I was convinced . . ." he said, "you could make your body do a great deal more than it seemed capable of doing."[2]

After graduating from college, Auerbach worked as a counselor at a juvenile correctional institution, then as a high school coach and teacher. After three years in the Navy during World War II, he became coach of the Washington Capitols in the Basketball Association of America. Four years later, he was coaching the Boston Celtics.

At first, the Celtics were just an average team. Things began to change when Boston picked up Bob Cousy, one of the league's most exciting stars. He was one of the first players to make behind-the-back dribbling a regular part of his game.

The Celtics, Auerbach figured, needed just one more ingredient to become champions: "I had to have somebody who could get me the ball."[3] In 1956, he acquired Bill Russell, one of the game's most fearsome centers. Russell's rebounds, blocked shots, and scowling attitude intimidated the opposition.

The Jackie Robinson Foundation
"ROBIE"
Award for Achievement in Industry

presented to

RED AUERBACH

RED AUERBACH

Even though his coaching days are long gone, Red Auerbach is still recognized as one of the best ever.

Auerbach's strategy was simple. When the opposition tried to shoot, they had to get around Russell, who planted himself in the lane. If their shot missed, the big center would be there to grab the rebound and flip the ball to Cousy. The speedy forward charged downcourt, using his fancy dribbling and passing to move the ball in for an easy shot. With Boston, almost every possession looked like a fast break.

In the deciding game of the 1957 NBA Finals, with less than a minute left, Russell blocked a shot, then hit a basket to put Boston ahead of the St. Louis Hawks, 102–101. The Hawks battled back, tying the game at the end of regulation and the first overtime. Finally, Boston's Jim Loscutoff's two free throws clinched a 125–123 victory. It was the Celtics' first championship.

An injury to Russell's ankle helped keep Boston from defending its title the next year. Then, starting with the 1958–59 season, Auerbach's teams won eight championships in a row. No other professional team has ever dominated a sport like the Celtics. No wonder fans of the other NBA teams got very tired of Auerbach's victory cigars.

Before the 1966–67 season, Auerbach announced that it would be his last as coach. In the playoffs, the Celtics whipped Wilt Chamberlain and the Philadelphia 76ers in just five games. Then, they dropped the Los Angeles Lakers in the Finals. The Boston fans went wild as Auerbach lit his final victory cigar.

Why was Auerbach the most successful coach in NBA history? Russell joked that the answer was simple: "He's versatile, he's intelligent, astute, flexible—and he has me on the team."

"I admire Russell," Auerbach said, "because he's smart enough to understand me."[4] When Auerbach retired, he moved to the Celtics' front office and made the big center Boston's new coach.

RED AUERBACH

BORN: September 20, 1917, Brooklyn, New York.

HIGH SCHOOL: Eastern District, Brooklyn, New York.

COLLEGE: Seth Low Junior College, George Washington University.

TEAMS COACHED: Washington Capitols, 1946–1949; Tri-Cities
Blackhawks, 1949–1950; Boston Celtics, 1950–1966.

CHAMPIONSHIPS: NBA, 1957, 1959–1966.

HONORS: NBA Coach of the Year, 1965. Elected to Naismith
Memorial Basketball Hall of Fame, 1968.

Red Auerbach was as well known for his victory cigars as he was
for his success on the court. The Boston Celtics won 9 NBA titles in
Auerbach's 16 years coaching the club.

CHUCK DALY

Chuck Daly was as aggressive on the sidelines as his Detroit Pistons were on the floor. The tough Pistons won back-to-back championships under Daly.

CHUCK DALY

MICHAEL JORDAN CALLED CHUCK DALY'S Detroit Pistons the dirtiest team in basketball.[1] Wayne Embry, the general manager of the Cleveland Cavaliers, called them "cheap-shot artists." He said, "They deliberately try to hurt people."[2]

Daly disagreed, of course. He said the Pistons made people mad because they played gutsy, aggressive basketball, and because they won. "It's difficult to keep running around screens and chasing your man, night after night, week after week, month after month. They did it, though, and when they found out it could make them successful, they kept on doing it."[3] The players liked their tough-guy image so much they called themselves the Bad Boys.

Chuck Daly had loved basketball since he was a little boy growing up in Kane, Pennsylvania. He always remembered the white leather basketball he and his brother, Bud, got when Chuck was twelve: "When you don't have much materially in life and suddenly you own such a treasure, you think you've died and gone to heaven. Bud and I couldn't believe it. Nobody in the world had a white basketball except the Daly brothers."[4]

By the time Daly became coach of the Detroit Pistons in 1983, he had decades of experience running teams on the high school, college, and pro levels, but he had never won a championship. To make it to the top of the NBA, he decided to build his team around Isiah Thomas, a young, six-foot one-inch, star guard.

By 1987, the Pistons were ready to challenge the league's best teams. They might have beaten the Boston Celtics in the Eastern Conference Finals, but they lost two of their best players in the seventh game when Adrian Dantley and Vinnie Johnson bumped heads while diving for a loose ball. The Celtics took the game, 117–114.

The next year, Daly's team made it past Boston before facing the Los Angeles Lakers in the Finals. Leading three games to two, the Pistons needed just one more win. Then, in the third quarter, Thomas suffered a severe ankle sprain. Somehow, he kept playing, limping up and down the court and firing up the team with eleven points in just four minutes. But two late free throws by Kareem Abdul-Jabbar gave the Lakers a 103–102 victory. In the deciding game, Los Angeles dropped the Pistons, 108–105.

In 1989, nobody could stop the Bad Boys. The Celtics fell in the first round. Jordan and the Chicago Bulls lost in the Eastern Conference Finals. Magic Johnson, Abdul-Jabbar, Coach Pat Riley, and the rest of the two-time champion Lakers were waiting. Would Detroit run out of steam again? Not a chance! The Pistons buried them in four straight.

The 1990 Finals clincher against the Portland Trail Blazers was tied, 90–90, with time running out. Vinnie Johnson told his teammates, "Gimme the rock!"[5] He took the pass and went up with a jumper just before the buzzer. On the bench, Daly's stomach did flip-flops. Nothing but net! "Back to back, baby!" the Pistons screamed.[6]

Daly said the Bad Boys were special: "Teams win championships, not individuals. The players must have ability, but . . . they have to be unselfish, and it's hard to find unselfish players."[7]

"Chuck Daly was the perfect coach for us," Thomas said. "He realized this team was something special, and it seemed as if he pressed the right buttons."[8]

Chuck Daly

BORN: July 20, 1930, St. Marys, Pennsylvania.

HIGH SCHOOL: Kane Area, Pennsylvania.

COLLEGE: St. Bonaventure University, Bloomsburg University of Pennsylvania.

TEAMS COACHED: Cleveland Cavaliers, 1981–1982; Detroit Pistons, 1983–1992; New Jersey Nets, 1992–1994; Orlando Magic, 1997– .

CHAMPIONSHIPS: NBA, 1989, 1990.

HONORS: Led United States Olympic Basketball Team to the gold medal in 1992 Olympics.

In 1992, Chuck Daly was chosen to coach the United States Olympic Men's Basketball Team. Known as the Dream Team, the United States cruised to the gold medal.

ALEX HANNUM

ALEX HANNUM WAS NOT MUCH of a basketball player: "I was never anything more than a journeyman player in the pros. The most I ever averaged was 7.5 points a game and the most I ever made was $9,000 a year. Near the end I just hung on because I was hooked. I loved basketball and I loved the life."[1]

Hannum might not have had much talent, but he was tough, even after his playing days were over. In 1963, Hannum was coach of the San Francisco Warriors, and Wilt Chamberlain was his star center. When the two men had a loud disagreement at practice, they had to be separated by other players.

Hannum liked his teams to be tough, too. Two powerful forwards, Bob Pettit and Cliff Hagan, formed the backbone of the St. Louis Hawks. In 1958, Hannum coached the team to a Finals encounter with the Boston Celtics. The Hawks won three of the first five games by a combined total of just seven points.

In the sixth game, Pettit really came through. He scored 50 points in the game. His final basket, a tip-in with fifteen seconds to go, sealed a 110–109 victory and the NBA title. It would be another nine years before another team would beat the Celtics in the Finals. "At the time, the Hawks were the most intense rivalry we had," said Boston great Bob Cousy. "They were tough."[2]

Hannum moved on to coach the San Francisco Warriors in 1963. It was there that he had his confrontation with Chamberlain. No punches were actually thrown, and soon the two men had a healthy respect for each other.

ALEX HANNUM

Alex Hannum is the only coach to ever win NBA titles with two different teams.

Chamberlain was a scoring machine; he had hit 100 points in a single game in 1962. In the two seasons before Hannum took over the Warriors, Wilt had averaged 48 points per game.

Hannum convinced Chamberlain to move the ball around. If he would concentrate more on blocking shots, rebounding, and passing to his teammates, San Francisco would be a stronger team. The strategy worked; Chamberlain's scoring average fell to 36.9, but the team won the Western Division. It was what Hannum called a "muscle and hustle team."[3] However, the Warriors were knocked off by the Celtics in the five-game Finals.

Three years later, Hannum and Chamberlain were together again, this time with the Philadelphia 76ers. They finished the season with 68 victories. Wilt "the Stilt" Chamberlain averaged only 24.1 points per game that season, but the team averaged 125.1. While sharing the scoring load, he was able to lead the league in rebounds (24.2).

In the opener of the Eastern Division Finals, Chamberlain outscored Bill Russell, 32–15, as Philadelphia whipped Boston, 127–113. After the 76ers won the second game, Chamberlain's rebounding, and some key baskets by Hal Greer and Wali Jones brought Philly a 115–104 win in Game 3. After losing, 121–117, to Boston, Hannum's team clinched the series with a convincing 140–116 victory. Then, in the Finals, the 76ers took out San Francisco in six games.

In 1968, Hannum jumped to the new American Basketball Association (ABA), where he took the Oakland Oaks to the league championship. He and Bill Sharman were the only coaches to win titles in both the ABA and NBA.

Alex Hannum is also the only coach to win NBA titles with two different teams. No other coach ever beat Red Auerbach's Celtics in the NBA Finals. No other coach ever won a playoff series against a Boston team with Bill Russell; Hannum did it twice.

ALEX HANNUM

BORN: July 19, 1923, Los Angeles, California.
HIGH SCHOOL: Hamilton, Los Angeles, California.
COLLEGE: University of Southern California.
TEAMS COACHED: St. Louis Hawks, 1956–1958; Syracuse Nationals, 1960–1963; San Francisco Warriors, 1963–1966; Philadelphia 76ers, 1966–1968; Oakland Oaks (ABA), 1968–1969; San Diego Rockets, 1969–1971; Denver Rockets (ABA), 1971–1974.
CHAMPIONSHIPS: NBA, 1958, 1967; ABA, 1969.
HONORS: NBA Coach of the Year, 1964; ABA Coach of the Year, 1969.

Alex Hannum was never one to be pushed around by his players. He even stood up to star center Wilt Chamberlain.

RED HOLZMAN

BASKETBALL NEVER SEEMED LIKE a very complicated game to Red Holzman. "See the ball! See the ball!" he screamed over and over. He always wanted his players to be alert and aware of where the action was going. His other rule was "Hit the open man!"[1] He believed that a good team doesn't care who scores.

Whether he was playing or coaching, Holzman always figured that the team with the best defense usually wins. "On offense, you guys can do what you want," he joked to his players. "But on defense you do what I want."[2] He expected his players to sweat. "Practices . . . will be mostly drill, repetition, and defense," he told the New York Knicks when he took over the team in 1968. "It's going to be hard work for you and for me, but if we win, it'll all be worth it."[3]

Bill Bradley was one of Holzman's favorite players because he always played all out. Bradley was sick in the locker room before one important game, but refused to sit out. "The team needs me, Red," he said. Bradley played a fine game, but after a while, Holzman tried to avoid time-outs "because each time he came back to the huddle he vomited. The stuff got on my shoes."[4]

With three seconds left in Game 3 of the 1970 NBA Finals, the Knicks led the Los Angeles Lakers, 102–100. Jerry West tossed up a 60-foot desperation shot that dropped in as the buzzer sounded—tie game! The miracle shot might have knocked the wind out of another squad, but not Holzman's Knicks. "This game's not over!" Dick Barnett told his teammates. "It's just starting!"[5] He was right; New York won a 111–108 thriller.

During his coaching career, Red Holzman stressed that defense was the most important part of the game.

RED HOLZMAN

Two games later, Willis Reed, the great Knicks center, went down with a torn thigh muscle. At halftime, with the team behind by thirteen, Bradley suggested a zone offense. The strategy worked, and New York won, 107–100.

After the Lakers took an easy 135–113 victory, the Knicks knew they had to have Reed in action for the decisive seventh game. Just before tipoff, Holzman escorted the center out of the locker room. The crowd at Madison Square Garden went berserk. "He gave us a tremendous lift just going out there," Holzman said.[6]

Reed couldn't even jump for the tipoff against Wilt Chamberlain, but he sank his first two shots. Somehow, playing on just one good leg, Reed limited Chamberlain to just two of nine shots. The rest of the Knicks, inspired by Reed's brave efforts, played incredible basketball. At the half, they led, 61–37; the Lakers were finished. Soon New York was celebrating its first NBA title.

Two years later, the Knicks met the Lakers again in the Finals. This time, with Reed out of action because of a knee injury, Chamberlain was overpowering, and Los Angeles won, four games to one.

In 1973, some Lakers said they wanted to face the Knicks, not a tough team like Boston. When Holzman's men nipped the Celtics in the Eastern Conference Finals, Walt Frazier told his Knick teammates, "They wanted us. They got us. Let's give them something to remember."[7] That was just the kind of talk Holzman liked to hear: "I felt pretty good about our chances after the Boston series. The team had a lot of intensity; we were at our peak."[8] The Knicks rolled over the Lakers in just five games.

New York players and fans still remember Red Holzman's years as coach. Dave DeBusschere, one of his star forwards, said, "It was a warm, wonderful time."[9]

RED HOLZMAN

BORN: August 10, 1920, Brooklyn, New York.

HIGH SCHOOL: Franklin K. Lane, Brooklyn, New York.

COLLEGE: Baltimore University, City College of New York.

TEAMS COACHED: Milwaukee/St. Louis Hawks, 1953–1957; New York Knicks, 1967–1982.

CHAMPIONSHIPS: NBA, 1970, 1973.

HONORS: NBA Coach of the Year, 1970; Elected to Naismith Memorial Basketball Hall of Fame, 1985.

Red Holzman congratulates star player Walt Frazier on making a game-winning shot. Holzman led the New York Knicks to NBA titles in 1970 and 1973.

PHIL JACKSON

Phil Jackson used a calm, relaxed style with the Chicago Bulls. The team responded, winning more championships in the 1990s than any other team.

WHEN HE WAS IN HIGH SCHOOL, Phil Jackson's friends called him "Bones" because he was so thin. By the time he was the popular sixth man on the New York Knicks, his arms were long enough to open both front doors of a car at the same time—while sitting in the backseat! On the basketball court, he used the elbows on his long arms to fight for position.

In 1987, when Jackson became an assistant coach for the Chicago Bulls, he was amazed by Michael Jordan, the team's young star guard: "Michael was blocking shots, he was rebounding, he was stealing; he was all over the place. It was a one-on-five match up, Michael against the opposition."[1]

Two years later, Jackson became the Bulls' head coach. He said he would copy the simple advice of his old coach, Red Holzman: "Hit the open man, see the ball and get back on defense. You'll see a team using speed and quickness."[2]

Jackson did not want the Bulls to be a one-man team. He adopted the triple-post offense designed by his assistant, Tex Winter. The Bulls would try to move the ball around, making their opponents keep an eye on everybody, not just Jordan.

The strategy worked. Chicago came within a game of beating the defending champs, the Detroit Pistons, in the 1990 Eastern Conference Finals. By then, the Bulls knew that Jackson had a unique coaching style; he didn't yell a lot or try to embarrass or bully his players. Before games, his pep talks were simple: "Do what we prepared you to do."[3] The coach didn't get rattled. Even when the pressure was on, he sat calmly on the bench, smiling at his players. He wanted them to know he was confident and that they should be, too.

Of course, despite the strategy and the preparation, sometimes the team played poorly. Once, when the team wasn't following his directions, Jackson called a time-out and stood silently, staring at his players. "The message was pretty clear," said John Bach, an assistant coach. "You're not listening, so solve it yourself."[4]

The next season, Chicago destroyed the Pistons in four straight playoff games. Then came a Finals matchup between the Bulls and the Los Angeles Lakers. After dropping the first game, Chicago took four in a row.

The Bulls made it three consecutive championships by beating Portland in 1992 and the Phoenix Suns a year later. Then, Jordan retired from basketball and began playing minor-league baseball. Without their superstar, Jackson's team was knocked out in the second round of the 1994 playoffs. In 1995, even after Jordan rejoined the squad, Chicago was again eliminated in the second round.

Before the next season, the Bulls gambled by signing Dennis Rodman. Many fans figured Rodman's bad attitude made him almost worthless as a player. But Rodman got along fine with Jackson and the Chicago players.

With Jordan, Scottie Pippen, and Rodman leading the way, the Bulls cruised to an NBA record-breaking 72–10 regular season. In the playoffs, they lost just three out of eighteen games, and Jackson had his fourth NBA title in just seven years. "This has been the easiest year of coaching I've ever had in my life," he said.[5] The Bulls added a fifth title in 1997.

Jordan, considered by many to be the finest basketball player ever, gave Phil Jackson a lot of credit: "Phil has taught me how to understand my teammates and give them a chance to gel and improve."[6]

Phil Jackson

BORN: September 17, 1945, Deer Lodge, Montana.
HIGH SCHOOL: Willison, North Dakota.
COLLEGE: University of North Dakota.
TEAMS COACHED: Chicago Bulls, 1989– .
CHAMPIONSHIPS: NBA, 1991–1993, 1996, 1997.
HONORS: NBA Coach of the Year, 1996.

Phil Jackson was able to unite a team of superstars into one cohesive unit. He brought great talents such as Michael Jordan (pictured with Jackson), Scottie Pippen, and Dennis Rodman together to create a winning combination.

JOHN KUNDLA

THE FIRST GREAT COACH OF THE NBA was a quiet man who worked in Minnesota. John Kundla won five of the league's first eight championships as coach of the Minneapolis Lakers.

It was a job he had not really wanted. He was a coach for St. Thomas College in St. Paul, Minnesota, in 1947, when Sid Hartman was trying to put together a professional team in nearby Minneapolis. After being turned down by several other coaches, Hartman asked Kundla to run the team. At first the young coach was not interested. Why should he leave a job he enjoyed?

Finally, he gave in. Maybe it would be fun to run a pro team. "Kundla was young and had nothing to lose, so he took the job," said Vern Mikkelsen, a Lakers forward.[1]

Fortunately, the Lakers also signed George Mikan, basketball's first superstar. He was a six-foot ten-inch giant with dark wavy hair and thick glasses. A deadly shooter who used his height and long arms to harass opponents and block their shots, Mikan played best under pressure. In close games, when Minneapolis needed a basket, he usually told Kundla, "Let me have the ball. I'll get it done."[2]

Because Big George Mikan wasn't a quick runner, his coach could not rely on the fast break. The Lakers usually ran a pick-and-roll play, which gave Mikan plenty of opportunity to score. "It was a simple little play," Kundla said. "But it was very successful."[3]

The Minneapolis Lakers were the first team capable of dunking the ball on almost every possession. Of the five starters, only one couldn't get high enough to dunk.

JOHN KUNDLA

Hall of Fame coach John Kundla was the first coach of the Minneapolis Lakers. He immediately brought the team success, winning six titles in twelve years, including five NBA championships.

However, the rest of them hardly ever did it, either. "Kundla wouldn't let us," said Mikkelsen. "It was frowned on as hot dogging."[4] The coach didn't want to embarrass the other teams.

Many of the other NBA squads didn't figure they had a chance with Mikan in the lineup. Throughout his career, he was punished with hard fouls. In the 1949 NBA Finals, Kleggie Hermsen of the Washington Capitols knocked the big center into the first row of seats. It wasn't just a foul, Mikan said; it felt like a tackle. He had to leave the game with a broken wrist.

Mikan came back wearing a cast. He kept scoring, and Kundla's men took the championship, four games to two.

The next year, in the Finals, the fans of the Syracuse Nationals came up with a new strategy to beat Mikan. Early in the series, newspapers reported that he was allergic to smoke. "That next night all the fans came out smoking cigars," he said. "You could hardly see across the floor," Kundla remembered. "It was filled with smoke."[5]

A broken wrist hadn't stopped Minneapolis's superstar; neither did the smoke. The Lakers won the title in six games. Kundla's teams also won championships in 1952, 1953, and 1954.

Only Red Auerbach of the Boston Celtics has won more titles than Kundla. But Kundla never received much recognition. Many reporters and fans seem to feel that with all the talent the Lakers had, it didn't take much coaching to win games. Auerbach disagreed. "Sure Kundla had a great team, but he did great things with them."[6]

The Lakers' first coach didn't seem to let the lack of recognition bother him. "Coaches don't win games and championships," he said. "Players do. The thing I'm most proud of is that I didn't blow it."[7]

JOHN KUNDLA

BORN: July 3, 1916, Star Junction, Pennsylvania.

HIGH SCHOOL: Central, Minneapolis, Minnesota.

COLLEGE: University of Minnesota.

TEAMS COACHED: Minneapolis Lakers, 1947–1959.

CHAMPIONSHIPS: NBL, 1948; NBA, 1949, 1950, 1952–1954.

HONORS: Elected to Naismith Memorial Basketball Hall of Fame, 1995.

Kundla (right) is shown here with Hall of Famer Elgin Baylor.

DON NELSON

Few players or coaches have ever had a knowledge of the game like Don Nelson. Here he is shown calling a play in to his team.

WHEN HE STARTED HIGH SCHOOL in Rock Island, Illinois, Don Nelson was miserable. "He was picked on a lot," said his son, Donnie. "He had big feet, and kids made fun of him." The only thing he liked about school was basketball. "The high school coach took him under his wing, and Dad poured himself into it. He found a release in basketball."[1]

Nelson was on some great teams, but he was never considered a superstar. "Don was the slowest guy I ever played with," said teammate JoJo White, "but his knowledge of the game was phenomenal."[2] Phil Jackson, then a forward with the New York Knicks, claimed that Nelson used a sticky substance to improve his game. "His hands are so sticky that he is able to palm the ball easily and fake opponents out . . . with his pump move."[3]

Nelson has used his knowledge of the game to become one of the winningest coaches in NBA history. However, despite ranking in the top ten in total victories, none of his teams has ever won a league title. In fact, none of them has even made it to the Finals.

During his many seasons with the Milwaukee Bucks, Golden State Warriors, Knicks, and Dallas Mavericks, Nelson has earned much respect from reporters, fans, and players. Nelson and Pat Riley are the only coaches to have been named NBA Coach of the Year three times.

"I loved playing for him," said Mike Dunleavy, a guard with the Bucks and later a coach with Milwaukee and the Los Angeles Lakers. "He was very demanding, and you had to get things right, but he made you a better player."[4] "He's a great teacher," said Golden State star Chris Mullin. "We're always learning and that makes it fun."[5]

During his ten years in Milwaukee, the Bucks won seven straight division titles, but always got bumped out of the playoffs before the Finals. Only in 1983, 1984, and 1986 did the Bucks even make it to the Eastern Conference Finals. In 1983 they fell to Julius Erving and the Philadelphia 76ers. In both 1984 and 1986 they were whipped by Larry Bird and the Celtics.

Nelson was able to mold the Bucks into a good team, but not a great one. They always seemed to be at least a superstar away from being able to win the big games from powerhouse teams like the Celtics and the Lakers.

It seemed to be the same story when Nelson moved to the Warriors in 1988. By the 1991–92 season, the team posted a 55–27 record, and he was again named Coach of the Year. Sadly, Golden State was eliminated from the playoffs in the first round by the Seattle SuperSonics.

In 1993, the Warriors picked up Chris Webber, the All-American forward who had led the University of Michigan to a pair of NCAA championship games. "He has the mental and physical capacities to be a great player." Nelson said. "He can't miss."[6] At last, he hoped, he had the big man he had always needed.

After winning Rookie of the Year Honors in 1994, Webber got tired of playing for Nelson. "Just treat me like a man!" he screamed at his coach.[7] Many fans supported Nelson, but no matter who was at fault, neither man found success with the Warriors. Webber was traded to the Washington Bullets in 1995, and Nelson was fired soon after.

The Knicks hired Nelson as their head coach in 1995, and then fired him less than a year later. The Dallas Mavericks then signed him to be their general manager. He took over as head coach in December 1997.

DON NELSON

BORN: May 15, 1940, Muskegon, Michigan.

HIGH SCHOOL: Rock Island, Illinois.

COLLEGE: University of Iowa.

TEAMS COACHED: Milwaukee Bucks, 1976–1987; Golden State Warriors, 1988–1995; New York Knicks, 1995–1996; Dallas Mavericks, 1997– .

HONORS: NBA Coach of the Year, 1983, 1985, 1992.

Don Nelson had a frustrating time with forward Chris Webber at Golden State. The two did not get along, and both would soon leave the Warriors for other NBA teams.

PAT RILEY

Pat Riley achieved success with the first team he coached in the NBA. The Los Angeles Lakers won four NBA championships with Riley as coach.

PAT RILEY SHOWED UP for his first high school varsity basketball practice with a cigarette dangling between his lips. His coach, Walt Pazybylo, slapped it out of his mouth. Over the next few months, "he really turned me around," Riley said.[1] Instead of trying to be a tough guy or a troublemaker, Riley began to concentrate on basketball.

As soon as he was hired as the Lakers' coach in 1981, Riley gained a reputation as a no-nonsense boss. He had a veteran superstar in Kareem Abdul-Jabbar, and Magic Johnson was a young guard in his third season. With the rest of the team, they got used to sweating through hours of drills at practice.

The hard work paid off. The rookie coach guided the Lakers to a victory in the NBA Finals against the Philadelphia 76ers in 1982.

In 1984, the Lakers ran into Larry Bird and the Boston Celtics in the Finals. The Celtics were an aggressive team that dove for loose balls and weren't afraid to give rough fouls. Riley called them "a bunch of thugs"; Los Angeles lost, four games to three.[2]

When the two teams met in the 1985 Finals, Riley had the Lakers play much more aggressively. "We're not out to physically harm them," Abdul-Jabbar explained. "But I wouldn't mind hurting their feelings."[3] Even though he was thirty-eight years old, Abdul-Jabbar averaged 26 points a game in the Finals, taking his team to a six-game victory.

Two years later, Riley had Los Angeles rely more on Johnson and James Worthy for its scoring punch. The strategy worked; Johnson averaged 23.9 points a game, and the

Lakers met the Celtics again in the Finals. With the Lakers down 106–105, Johnson dribbled in, then stopped, as Bird, Robert Parish, and Kevin McHale jumped up to block his hook shot. The ball went over their hands and through the hoop, with just two seconds left. The Lakers won, 107–106! In the title-clinching sixth game, Los Angeles buried Boston, 106–93.

After the 1987 Finals, reporters asked Riley if his team could win it all again in 1988. The coach shocked almost everybody by saying, "I guarantee it."[4] Was he crazy? A guarantee like that put an enormous amount of pressure on his players, but Riley knew what he was doing. "Pro players demand discipline. . . ." he said. "But I spend even more of my time thinking about how to motivate players."[5]

In 1988, it took them seven games to do it, but the Lakers made good on his guarantee by beating the Detroit Pistons in the Finals. "'Riles' did a great job for us," Worthy said. The guarantee had made the team "mentally alert" and "focused."[6]

By that time, Riley was almost as famous as his superstars. The actor Michael Douglas even copied the coach's slicked-back hairstyle in the movie *Wall Street*.[7]

After nine seasons with Los Angeles, Riley quit in 1990 to become a broadcaster, but a year later, he took over the New York Knicks. In 1994, his new team lost in the Finals to the Houston Rockets in seven games. After four seasons with New York, Riley switched to the Miami Heat in 1995, and he was named Coach of the Year in 1997.

No matter the team, Pat Riley has remained one of the most well-known—and successful—coaches in the NBA. Magic Johnson spoke for many athletes when he said, "You would go through a wall for him."[8]

PAT RILEY

BORN: March 20, 1945, Rome, New York.

HIGH SCHOOL: Linton High School, Schenectady, New York.

COLLEGE: University of Kentucky.

TEAMS COACHED: Los Angeles Lakers, 1981–1990; New York Knicks, 1991–1995; Miami Heat, 1995– .

CHAMPIONSHIPS: NBA, 1982, 1985, 1987, 1988.

HONORS: NBA Coach of the Year, 1990, 1993, 1997.

Pat Riley left Los Angeles in 1990, but soon returned to coach the New York Knicks. In 1995, Riley took over as head coach and team president of the Miami Heat.

BILL RUSSELL

Bill Russell not only played for the Celtics during the 1966–67 season, but also was the team's coach. This task would prove difficult, and Russell could not bring his team to a ninth consecutive NBA title.

BILL RUSSELL

WHEN HE WAS A KID IN OAKLAND, California, Bill
Russell was not good enough to make his junior high school
team. At McClymonds High, he barely made the junior
varsity team. It wasn't until he got older and bigger that he
became a star for the school's varsity squad.

Russell has always figured that basketball kept him
"from becoming a juvenile delinquent."[1] The sport kept
him out of trouble and made him nationally famous when
he led the University of San Francisco to the NCAA championships in 1955 and 1956.

After years of playing under Coach Red Auerbach for the
Boston Celtics, Russell became player-coach, the first
African-American coach in NBA history. Before the 1966–67
season began, he told the veterans on his team that he knew
very little about coaching and that he would welcome their
suggestions. At practices, he didn't work them very hard.

The new coach didn't give pep talks or scream at his players. When his men were hurt, he helped them off the court.
"You see," he said, "first these men are my friends."[2]

Russell led the team by example. "He wasn't ever the
rah-rah type," said forward Bailey Howell. "He just led the
team with the way he played. . . . He was at his best in crucial games. . . . Then you'd rather have Bill Russell on your
side than anybody."[3]

With so much experience in pressure situations,
Russell's teams stayed calm when other teams lost their
cool. They stuck together as a team, never seeming to care
about individual statistics as long as they kept winning.

But in Russell's rookie season as coach, Boston lost in

the second round of the 1967 playoffs to the Philadelphia 76ers. The Celtic fans booed Russell.

A year later, Boston and Philadelphia met again in the playoffs. "We're not supposed to win anything," Russell told his team. "Stay loose and just go out there and play the way you can."[4] In the seventh and deciding game, the 76ers trailed, 98–96, but they had the ball, with time running out. Philadelphia's Chet Walker drove for a shot, but Russell blocked it! Hal Greer grabbed the ball, but his shot missed. When Russell snatched the rebound, Philly was finished.

Then the Celtics knocked off the Los Angeles Lakers, four games to two, in the Finals. As the last seconds ticked off, Russell joyously hugged teammate John Havlicek. "He is an unbelievable man," marveled Jerry West of the Lakers.[5]

Boston finished the 1968–69 regular season fourth in the Eastern Division. In one of the final games of the season, the Celtics were whipped by the Lakers, 108–73. Russell was furious, and he made a rare speech to his team. Where was their pride? Were they ready to give up?

The playoffs were another story. Somehow, Russell guided his men to a seventh-game Finals showdown against Los Angeles. The Lakers' management hung thousands of balloons in the rafters of the Forum. When their team won, the balloons would be dropped.

Boston ruined the party. With a minute to go, Celtic Don Nelson grabbed a loose ball and heaved a shot that put the Celtics up for good, 105–102. The final score was 108–106, and Russell had his second straight championship.

Bill Russell was a great coach for the same reason that he was a great player. As a reporter wrote in 1963, "The foundation of Russell's brilliant play is not blocking shots, rebounding or his other purely physical skills. It is, rather, his admirable mind and purpose, his intelligence . . . and his pride."[6]

BILL RUSSELL

BORN: February 12, 1934, Monroe, Louisiana.

HIGH SCHOOL: McClymonds High School, Oakland, California.

COLLEGE: University of San Francisco.

TEAMS COACHED: Boston Celtics, 1966–1969; Seattle SuperSonics, 1973–1977; Sacramento Kings, 1987–1988.

CHAMPIONSHIPS: NBA, 1968, 1969.

HONORS: First African American to be named the head coach of a major sports team; Elected to Naismith Memorial Basketball Hall of Fame, 1974.

Russell loved the game and was one of the best players ever. As a coach, he won two NBA championships, in 1967–68 and 1968–69.

RUDY TOMJANOVICH

In Rudy Tomjanovich's second full season of coaching, he led the Houston Rockets to a seven-game victory over the New York Knickerbockers to win the 1994 NBA championship.

RUDY TOMJANOVICH

WHEN HE WAS CUT from his high school freshman basketball team, Rudy Tomjanovich was so angry he challenged his coach to a game of one-on-one. It was a one-sided match; Rudy T was whipped badly. "I was a skinny kid," he said, "but he saw that I really wanted to be on the team, so he gave me a uniform."[1]

Eventually Tomjanovich became good enough to be selected All-American at the University of Michigan. He joined the Houston Rockets in 1970 as a forward.

In 1992–93, his first full season as coach of the Rockets, Tomjanovich guided them to the top of the Central Division. His secret? He treated his players with respect and expected them to play extremely tough defense. That year they made it all the way to the Western Conference Semifinals, which they lost to the Seattle SuperSonics in seven games.

Houston won the division the next season, then ripped the Portland Trail Blazers, Phoenix Suns, and Utah Jazz to earn a spot in the Finals against Pat Riley's New York Knicks. Many observers wondered how Rudy T would stand up against Riley, the man who had coached Los Angeles to four titles, then made the Knicks contenders again. After all, in 1994, Tomjanovich was finishing up only his second full season as a head coach.

New York, in fact, came within a shot of taking the title in just six games. Down 86–84, John Starks of the Knicks took a pass in three-point territory. As the final seconds ticked off, he released a long shot. Hakeem Olajuwon, Houston's magnificent center, lunged at the ball, slapping it out of bounds as the buzzer sounded. The Rockets had forced a seventh game!

In the finale, an early Houston lead was eroded by steady Knicks shooting. New York was within three, 78–75, when Olajuwon dropped in a jumper. After Patrick Ewing missed a jumper of his own, Vernon Maxwell sank the clincher, a three-pointer with 1:48 to go. Rudy T raised his arms into the air as the Rockets mobbed Maxwell. The final was 90–84; it was the Rockets' first NBA championship. "Houston, you've wanted it for so long," the happy coach said. "You've finally got it."[2]

Hardly anybody gave the Rockets a chance to repeat in 1995. After a mediocre 47–35 record, they were seeded sixth in the conference playoffs. But Tomjanovich convinced his players they were as good as any other team in the league. They edged the Jazz and Suns before beating the San Antonio Spurs.

In the Finals, Houston was up against the Orlando Magic, a young, exciting team led by Shaquille O'Neal. In the first game, the Magic led by as much as twenty points before the Rockets battled back. With 1.6 seconds left in regulation, Kenny Smith's three-pointer tied the game. In overtime, Olajuwon tapped in a rebound with less than a second to go, to give Houston a 120–118 victory. "We have a big heart," Tomjanovich told reporters. "This team never gives up."[3]

The Rockets took the next two games, 117–106 and 106–103. Then Olajuwon put Shaq and the Magic away with 35 points and 15 rebounds, as Houston won, 113–101. "Don't underestimate the heart of a champion," Tomjanovich said. "I'm the proudest guy in the world."[4]

"There are probably people . . . who are wondering how we ever turned into a championship team," Maxwell said. "Well, Rudy T is a big part of the answer."[5]

RUDY TOMJANOVICH

BORN: November 24, 1948, Hamtramck, Michigan.

HIGH SCHOOL: Hamtramck, Michigan.

COLLEGE: University of Michigan.

TEAMS COACHED: Houston Rockets, 1991– .

CHAMPIONSHIPS: NBA, 1994, 1995.

Critics doubted that Tomjanovich's Rockets could repeat. In 1995, the team proved them wrong by beating the Orlando Magic for a second straight NBA title.

CHAPTER NOTES

Red Auerbach

1. Gilbert Rogin, "They All Boo When Red Sits Down," *Sports Illustrated,* vol. 22, no. 14 April 5, 1965, p. 105.

2. Charles Moritz, ed., *Current Biography* (New York: H. W. Wilson Company, 1969), p. 20.

3. Billy Packer and Roland Lazenby, *The Golden Game* (Dallas: Taylor Publishing Company, 1991), p. 99.

4. Myron Cope, "A Last Cigar for a Last Hurrah?" *Saturday Evening Post,* vol. 239, March 26, 1966, p. 112.

Chuck Daly

1. Isiah Thomas with Matt Dobek, *Bad Boys!* (Grand Rapids, Mich.: Masters Press, 1989), p. 23.

2. Gene Myers, ed., *Bad Boys* (Detroit: Detroit Free Press, 1989), p. 10.

3. Chuck Daly with Joe Falls, *Daly Life* (Grand Rapids, Mich.: Masters Press, 1990), p. 283.

4. Ibid., p. 23.

5. Gene Myers, ed., *Encore!* (Detroit: Detroit Free Press, 1990), p. 101.

6. Ibid.

7. Daly, p. 282.

8. Thomas, p. 231.

Alex Hannum

1. Alex Hannum with Frank Deford, "I've Barely Begun to Fight," *Sports Illustrated,* vol. 29, November 18, 1968, p. 34.

2. Billy Packer and Roland Lazenby, *The Golden Game* (Dallas: Taylor Publishing Company, 1991), p. 108.

3. Roland Lazenby, *The NBA Finals* (Dallas: Taylor Publishing Company, 1990), p. 92.

Red Holzman

1. Red Holzman and Harvey Frommer, *Red on Red* (New York: Bantam Books, 1975), p. 67.

2. Roland Lazenby, *The NBA Finals* (Dallas: Taylor Publishing Company, 1990), p. 123.

3. Holzman and Frommer, p. 61.

4. Ibid., p. 77.

5. Lazenby, p. 127.

6. Ibid., p. 129.

7. Holzman and Frommer, p. 140.

8. Ibid.

9. Billy Packer and Roland Lazenby, *The Golden Game* (Dallas: Taylor Publishing Company, 1991), p. 144.

Phil Jackson

1. Jeff Coplon, "The Age of Jackson," *New York Times* Magazine, May 17, 1992, p. 59.

2. Judith Graham, *Current Biography Yearbook* (New York: H. W. Wilson Company, 1992), p. 290.

3. Richard Hoffer, "Sitting Bull," *Sports Illustrated,* vol. 84, May 27, 1996, p. 84.

4. Ibid., p. 86.

5. Gary Hill, Reuter dispatch, June 11, 1996.

6. Ibid.

John Kundla

1. Roland Lazenby, *The Lakers: A Basketball Journey* (New York: St. Martin's Press, 1993), p. 85.
2. Ibid., pp. 69–70.
3. Ibid., p. 79.
4. Ibid.
5. Ibid., pp. 89–90.
6. Billy Packer and Roland Lazenby, *The Golden Game* (Dallas: Taylor Publishing Company, 1991), p. 83.
7. Roland Lazenby, *The NBA Finals* (Dallas: Taylor Publishing Company, 1990), p. 37.

Don Nelson

1. Chris Smith, "Hoop Genius Don Nelson," *New York*, vol. 28, November 27, 1995, p. 54.
2. Ibid., pp. 53–54.
3. Phil Jackson with Charles Rosen, *Maverick* (Chicago: Playboy Press, 1975), p. 114.
4. Leigh Montville, "The Crash," *Sports Illustrated*, vol. 82, January 16, 1995, p. 40.
5. Golden State Warriors 1994–95 Media Guide, p. 15.
6. Ibid., p. 54.
7. Smith, p. 55.

Pat Riley

1. Charles Moritz, *Current Biography Yearbook* (New York: H. W. Wilson Company, 1988), p. 480.
2. Roland Lazenby, *The NBA Finals* (Dallas: Taylor Publishing Company, 1990), p. 219.
3. Ibid., p. 224.
4. Jack McCallum, "The Dread R Word," *Sports Illustrated*, vol. 68, April 18, 1988, p. 51.
5. Michael Rozek, "What Does a Coach Do, Anyway?" *Sport*, March 1984, p. 36.
6. Moritz, p. 483.
7. Mark Heisler, *The Lives of Riley* (New York: Macmillan, 1994), p. 4.
8. Ibid.

Bill Russell

1. Charles Moritz, *Current Biography Yearbook* (New York: H. W. Wilson Company, 1988), p. 373.
2. Roland Lazenby, *The NBA Finals* (Dallas: Taylor Publishing Company, 1990), p. 117.
3. Ibid., p. 111.
4. Bob Ryan, *The Boston Celtics* (Reading, Mass.: Addison-Wesley Publishing Company, 1989), p. 49.
5. Lazenby, p. 114.
6. Gilbert Rogin, "We Are Grown Men Playing a Child's Game," *Sports Illustrated*, vol. 19, November 18, 1963, pp. 76–77.

Rudy Tomjanovich

1. Phil Taylor, "'Hey, Call Anytime,'" *Sports Illustrated*, vol. 81, July 4, 1994, p. 39.
2. Ibid.
3. Associated Press dispatch, June 22, 1994.
4. Gannett News Service dispatch, June 7, 1995.
5. Michael Lopresti, Gannett News Service dispatch, June 14, 1995.

INDEX